The Story of a Special Day
Volume 70

March 10

69th day of the year
(70th in leap years)
296 days remaining
until the end of the year.

by Michael Dobson

Timespinner
Press

Table of Contents

Cover: Photograph of a telephone, in honor of the first telephone call, March 10, 1876

Back Cover: The month of March, from the illuminated manuscript *Les Très Riches Heures du duc de Berry*

March 10 Quotations

"Mr. Watson, come here, I want to see you."

— Alexander Graham Bell, making the first telephone call on March 10, 1876

"I would not want to be a politician... Let me tell you this: If I was campaigning, and I go against my opponent and he started attacking my character, and I leap over the table and choke him unconscious, would that help my campaign?"

— Chuck Norris, born March 10, 1940

"Thinking people, when disaster strikes, make it their priority to look for its causes, in order to prevent it happening again."

— Osama bin Laden, born March 10, 1957

"I freed a thousand slaves. I could have freed a thousand more if only they knew they were slaves."

— Harriet Tubman, died March 10, 1913

First Telephone Call

It's one of the iconic moments of modern history: Alexander Graham Bell saying, "Mr. Watson, come here, I want to see you," followed by Watson's answer. The first two-way transmission of clear speech using a telephone took place on March 10, 1876.

Alexander Graham Bell was born in Scotland in 1847, and experimented with sound and speech in his teenage years, successfully building a lifelike head that could "speak." After the death of his younger brother, he emigrated with his parents to the United States. He learned the Mohawk language and developed a way to write it down, and worked with the deaf, most famously tutoring Helen Keller. He turned his talents toward transmitting the human voice over long distances, working with Thomas Watson, an electrical designer and mechanic to build the apparatus.

Although Alexander Graham Bell is commonly thought of as the inventor of the telephone, that's not entirely accurate. In 1833, German researchers Carl Gauß and Wilhelm Weber invented a way to transmit signals electrically. Italians credit Innocenzo Manzetti for the telephone's invention, somewhere around 1864 or 1865. Belgian Charles Bourseul invented an electromagnetic microphone, but couldn't turn the current back into sound.

The term "telephon" goes back to 1860, and German Johann Reis, who made a functioning telephone. (The first words spoken on it were *"Das Pferd frisst keinen Gurkensalat,"* or "The horse doesn't eat cucumber salad.") Thomas Edison tested the Reis instrument and found that it worked. Italian Antonio Meucci submitted a patent caveat for a "telettrofono" in 1871, but couldn't come up with the $10 fee to renew it. Other claimants include Englishman Cromwell Varley, Dane Poul la Cour, and American Daniel Drawbaugh.

American inventor Elisha Gray is the biggest claimant to the title. Both Gray and Bell filed their patent applications on the same day, and the controversy resulted in several lawsuits, all eventually resolved in favor of Bell.

Bell continued to invent throughout his life, winning eighteen patents. He developed the "photophone," which transmitted voice on a beam of light, the metal detector, and worked on hydrofoils and early airplanes. Bell died in 1922 at his private estate in Nova Scotia, where he is buried.

Alexander Graham Bell calling long distance, 1892.

March 10 Holidays and Celebrations

Hote Matsuri (Shiogama Shrine, Japan)

The "Sail-Cord Festival" is a Shinto sacred event that takes place on March 10 each year at Shiogama Shrine in Miyagi Prefecture, Japan. The festival began as a prayer for fire protection in 1682, but now involves praying for domestic safety and business prosperity.

Tibetan Uprising Day

Individuals and organizations who support Tibetan independence from China observe March 10 as a commemoration of the 1959 Tibetan uprising. It is often accompanied by a statement from the Dalai Lama. There have been riots and other disturbances in the Tibetan city of Lhasa associated with this event.

Christian Feast Days

Saints commemorated on March 10 include Anastasia the Patrician, Marie-Eugénie de Jésus, Himelin, John Oglivie, Macharius, and Pope Simplicius.

What Happened on March 10?

241 BC - Battle of the Aegates Islands

The First Punic War was the first of three wars fought between the Roman Republic and ancient Carthage. Rome won the first of these wars in the Battle of the Aegates Islands, March 10, 241 BC, located off the coast of Sicily, cutting off naval support to Carthaginian forces on the island and destroying the Carthaginian fleet.

1629 CE - Charles I Dissolves Parliament

The powers of England's Parliament had grown steadily for hundreds of years, but King Charles I, responding to increasing criticism of his rule, dissolved Parliament altogether for a period of eleven years, from 1629 to 1640. This is known as the "Personal Rule" or as the "Eleven Years' Tyranny" by Charles's enemies. Parliament came back into session in 1640, and two years later the English Civil War broke out.

Portrait of Charles I by Daniël Mijtens , 1632

1814 CE - Napoleon Defeated at Laon

Napoleon's France was defeated in Russia in 1812, and by 1814 was fighting for its very life. In the Battle of Laon, March 9-10, 1914, a combined Prussian and Russian force under Field Marshal Gebhard von Blücher defeated Napleon's army near Laon in northern France, clearing the way for the allied forces to advance on Paris.

1831 CE - French Foreign Legion Founded

King Louis Philippe of France founded the French Foreign Legion on March 10, 1831, to "remove disruptive elements from society and put them to use fighting the enemies of France." Although the Foreign Legion acquired a reputation as a "haven for cut-throats, crooks, and sundry fugitives from justice," today it is an elite arm of the French military with a strong *esprit de corps*.

1848 CE - Treaty of Guadalupe Hidalgo Ratified

The Treaty of Guadalupe Hidalgo, ratified by the U.S. Senate on March 10, 1848, ended the Mexican-American War (1846-1848), giving the United States control of Texas, California, New Mexico, Arizona, Nevada, Utah, and parts of Wyoming and Colorado. In Mexico, the war is known as *La Intervención Estadounidense* (the American Intervention).

1864 CE - American Civil War: The Red River Campaign Begins

From March 10 to May 22, 1864, 30,000 Union troops under the command of General Nathanial

Banks battled a force of 6,000-15,000 Confederates under the command of General Richard Taylor. Poor planning and mismanagement on the part of the Union allowed the far smaller Confederate force to defend the Red River Valley of Louisiana successfully.

Illustration of the Courrières mine disaster

1906 CE - Courrières Mine Disaster

The worst mining accident in European history (and the second-worst in world history) took place in northern France on March 10, 1906, killing 1,099 miners, including numerous children. The disaster resulted from an explosion of coal dust, but the cause of the initial ignition remains unknown.

1922 CE - **Gandhi Arrested**

The success of Mahatma Gandhi's "non-cooperation" campaign of peaceful resistance to British rule in India led to his arrest on March 10, 1922. He was tried for sedition and sentenced to six years' imprisonment, but was released after two years for an appendicitis operation.

Gandhi spinning, late 1920s

1933 CE - **Long Beach Earthquake**

Just before 6pm on March 10, 1933, a 6.4 magnitude earthquake rattled southern California, causing $50 million in property damage and killing 120 people. Because a number of school buildings collapsed (fortunately not during school hours), California passed the Field Act to make schools earthquake resistant.

1952 CE - Batista Becomes President of Cuba

Fulgencio Batista

Following the 1933 "Revolt of the Sergeants" in Cuba, Fulgencio Batista appointed himself chief of the armed forces. After ruling through a series of puppet presidents, Batista was elected President of Cuba in his own right, taking office on March 10, 1952. He fled the country on New Year's Day, 1959, after his forces were defeated by rebels under the command of Che Guevara at the Battle of Santa Clara, leading to the dictatorship of Fidel Castro.

1959 CE - Tibetan Uprising

On March 10, 1959, a revolt against Chinese rule of Tibet began in its capital city, Lhasa. Although armed resistance in eastern Tibet had been going on for several years, the rumor spread that the Chinese were about to take the Dalai Lama into custody. The conflict quickly grew, leading to a Chinese military response and the deaths of tens of thousands of Tibetans. The Dalai Lama fled into exile and the Chinese retained control of Tibet. Tibetan exiles honor March 10 as Tibetan Uprising Day.

1968 CE - Battle of Lima Site 85

Beginning on March 10, 1968, forces of the Vietnam People's Army attacked and captured a clandestine United States Air Force site in Laos, resulting in the largest USAF ground combat loss of the Vietnam War.

1969 CE - James Earl Ray Confesses

On March 10, 1969, James Earl Ray confessed to the assassination of Martin Luther King, Jr., in Memphis, Tennessee. He was sentenced to 99 years in prison. Ray subsequently recanted his confession, but was unable to secure a new trial.

WANTED BY THE FBI

CIVIL RIGHTS - CONSPIRACY
INTERSTATE FLIGHT - ROBBERY
JAMES EARL RAY

FBI No. 405,942 G

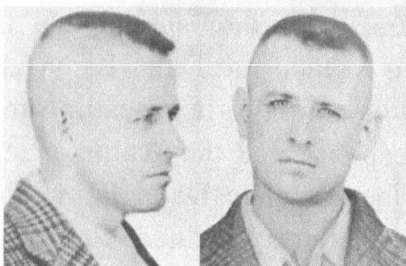

Photographs taken 1960

Photograph taken 1968
(eyes drawn by artist)

Aliases: Eric Starvo Galt, W. C. Herron, Harvey Lowmyer, James McBride, James O'Conner, James Walton, James Walyon, John Willard, "Jim,"

DESCRIPTION

Age:	40, born March 10, 1928, at Quincy or Alton, Illinois (not supported by birth records)		
Height:	5' 10"	**Eyes:**	Blue
Weight:	163 to 174 pounds	**Complexion:**	Medium
Build:	Medium	**Race:**	White
Hair:	Brown, possibly cut short	**Nationality:**	American

Occupations: Baker, color matcher, laborer

Scars and Marks: Small scar on center of forehead and small scar on palm of right hand

Remarks: Noticeably protruding left ear; reportedly is a lone wolf; allegedly attended dance instruction school; has reportedly completed course in bartending.

Fingerprint Classification: 16 M 9 U OOO 12

M 4 W I OI

CRIMINAL RECORD

Ray has been convicted of burglary, robbery, forging U. S. Postal Money Orders, armed robbery, and operating motor vehicle without owner's consent.

CAUTION

RAY IS SOUGHT IN CONNECTION WITH A MURDER WHEREIN THE VICTIM WAS SHOT. CONSIDER ARMED AND EXTREMELY DANGEROUS.

A Federal warrant was issued on April 17, 1968, at Birmingham, Alabama, charging Ray as Eric Starvo Galt with conspiring to interfere with a Constitutional Right of a citizen (Title 18, U. S. Code, Section 241). A Federal warrant was also issued on July 20, 1967, at Jefferson City, Missouri, charging Ray with Interstate Flight to Avoid Confinement for the crime of Robbery (Title 18, U. S. Code, Section 1073).

IF YOU HAVE ANY INFORMATION CONCERNING THIS PERSON, PLEASE NOTIFY ME OR CONTACT YOUR LOCAL FBI OFFICE. TELEPHONE NUMBERS AND ADDRESSES OF ALL FBI OFFICES LISTED ON BACK.

EXHIBIT II
TO THE AFFIDAVIT OF
CHARLES QUITMAN STEPHENS

DIRECTOR
FEDERAL BUREAU OF INVESTIGATION
UNITED STATES DEPARTMENT OF JUSTICE
WASHINGTON, D. C. 20535
TELEPHONE, NATIONAL 8-7117

Wanted Flyer 442-A
April 19, 1968

Wanted poster of James Earl Ray.

1977 CE - Rings of Uranus Discovered

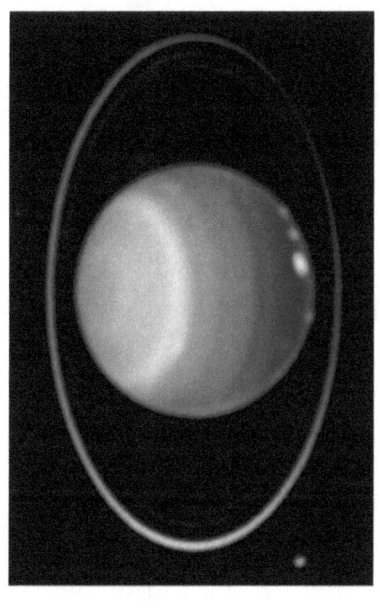

Astronomers James Elliot, Edward Dunham, and Douglas Mink discovered a system of rings, similar to those around Saturn, surrounding the planet Uranus, giving rise to innumerable grade school jokes. (The correct pronunciation is 'yŭr-ə-nəs, with the emphasis on the first syllable.)

1980 CE - Scarsdale Diet Doctor Murdered

On March 10, 1980, Jean Harris, headmistress of the Madeira School for Girls in Virginia, shot and killed her lover Dr. Herman Tarnower, better known as the "Scarsdale Diet Doctor." Her trial was a national sensation, and she was convicted and sentenced to 15 years to life. Her sentence was commuted in 1992 and she moved to a retirement home in Connecticut.

1990 CE - **Prosper Avril Ousted**

Prosper Avril, President of Haiti, led the 1988 military coup d'état and served as president until being ousted on March 10, 1990, a period described by Amnesty International as "marred by serious human rights violations." He was arrested in 2001 and released in 2004.

2006 CE - **Mars Reconnaissance Orbiter Reaches the Red Planet**

Launched in 2005, the Mars Reconnaissance Orbiter (MRO) entered orbit around the Red Planet on March 10, 2006. It monitors Mars' daily weather and surface conditions and will serve as a relay satellite for future missions.

Who Was Born on March 10?

The abbreviation "O.S." on some dates refers to the fact that the Russian Empire did not switch from the Julian to the Gregorian calendar at the same time as the rest of Europe, and therefore some figures have two dates for their birth or death.

People whose original names are not in the Western alphabet have their native names in the appropriate script shown in parenthesis.

Acting and Modeling

Olivia Wilde (March 10, 1984 —)

Actress and fashion model Olivia Wilde has appeared in numerous television series and movies, including *Tron: Legacy* and *Cowboys & Aliens*.

Edi Gathegi (March 10, 1979 —)

Kenyan-American actor Edi Gathegi had a recurring role on the TV series *House* and appeared as Laurent in the *Twilight* films.

Danny Pudi (March 10, 1979 —)

Danny Pudi played Abed Nadir on the NBC sitcom *Community*.

Rita Simons (March 10, 1977 —)

English actress Rita Simons is best known for her role in the long-running BBC soap opera *EastEnders*.

Jeff Branson (March 10, 1977 —)

American soap star Jeff Branson played long-running roles in *All My Children, Guiding Light,* and *The Young and the Restless*.

Eva Herzigová (March 10, 1973 —)

Czech model Eva Herzigová has modeled for Wonderbra, Guess? jeans, Victoria's Secret, and *Sports Illiustrated*.

Jon Hamm (March 10, 1971 —)

Actor Jon Hamm is best known for playing advertising executive Don Draper in the TV series *Mad Men*.

Jon Hamm

Jasmine Guy (March 10, 1962 —)

Actress Jasmine Guy is best known for her starring role in the TV sitcom *A Different World*.

Sharon Stone (March 10, 1958 —)

Sharon Stone is best known for her role in the erotic thriller *Basic Instinct,* and won a Golden Globe and an Academy Award nomination for her performance in *Casino.*

Shannon Tweed (March 10, 1957 —)

Erotic thriller star Shannon Tweed is married to Kiss singer Gene Simmons and appears in the reality show *Gene Simmons Family Jewels.*

Gloria Diaz (March 10, 1947 —)

Gloria Diaz, an award-winning actress in the Philippines, was the first Filipino named Miss Universe in 1969.

Katherine Houghton (March 10, 1945 —)

Katherine Houghton is best known for her role in the 1967 film *Guess Who's Coming to Dinner,* and has appeared in ten films. She is the niece of her *Dinner* co-star Katherine Hepburn.

Chuck Norris (March 10, 1940 —)

Martial artist and actor Chuck Norris starred in the TV series *Walker, Texas Ranger*, and became the focus of an Internet meme known as "Chuck Norris Facts."

Richard Haydn (March 10, 1905 — April 25, 1985)

English comic actor Richard Haydn voiced the Caterpillar in the 1951 Disney film *Alice in Wonderland* and played "Uncle Max" in the film *The Sound of Music*.

Business and Computers

Biz Stone (March 10, 1974 —)

Biz Stone co-founded and served as creative director of Twitter, Inc.

Bill Buxton (March 10, 1949 —)

Bill Buxton, a principal researcher at Microsoft, is one of the pioneers in the human-computer interaction field, winning the SIGCHI Lifetime Achievement Award in 2008.

Alfred Peet (March 10, 1920 — August 29, 2007)

Coffee roaster Alfred Peet founded Peet's Coffee and Tea and is known as "the Dutchman who taught America how to drink [custom] coffee."

Letters

Johanna Lindsey (March 10, 1952 —)

All of historical romance author Johanna Lindsey's many novels have made the *New York Times* bestseller list.

Bob Greene (March 10, 1947 —)

Award-winning newspaper columnist Bob Greene is the author of numerous nonfiction books. He was involved in a scandal with a 17-year old girl and was forced to leave the Chicago *Tribune.*

David Rabe (March 10, 1940 —)

Playwright David Rabe won the Tony Award for Best Play in 1972 for *Sticks and Bones,* and received three more nominations, most recently for 1985's *Hurlyburly*.

Music and Entertainment

Carrie Underwood (March 10, 1983 —)

Country music star Carrie Underwood won the fourth season of American Idol in 2005 and subsequently became a multiple Grammy winner and the Academy of Country Music's Entertainer of the Year. She has sold over 15 million albums.

Carrie Underwood

Robin Thicke (March 10, 1977 —)

Canadian singer-songrwiter Robin Thicke is the son of actor Alan Thicke. He has won numerous awards for his R&B work as recording artist and songwriter.

Timbaland (March 10, 1972 —)

Rapper Timbaland (Timothy Mosley) is known for his work producing such artists as Justin

Timberlake, Nelly Furtado, as well as for his solo work.

Daryle Singletary (March 10, 1971 —)

Country music singer Daryle Singeltary has had five hits on the Hot Country Songs Top 40.

Edie Brickell (March 10, 1966 —)

Edie Brickell and the New Bohemians first hit the charts with "What I Am" in 1988. She is married to musician Paul Simon.

Neneh Cherry (March 10, 1964 —)

Swedish singer-songwriter and rapper Neneh Cherry's first album *Raw Like Sushi* won a Brit Award and was nominated for a Grammy.

Lance Burton (March 10, 1960 —)

Stage magician Lance Burton performed over 5,000 shows for nearly 5 million people and grossed over $200 million in his 31 year career.

Ralph Emery (March 10, 1933 —)

Country music disc jockey and TV host Ralph Emery hosted the syndicated TV series *Pop! Goes the Country.*

Bix Beiderbecke (seated, right) with the Wolverine Orchestra

Bix Beiderbecke (March 10, 1903 — August 6, 1931)

One of the most influential jazz soloists of the 1920s, cornetist Bix Beiderbecke's brief life was the subject of the fictionalized semi-biography *Young Man With a Horn,* which became a 1950 film starring Kirk Douglas and Lauren Bacall.

Barry Fitzgerald (March 10, 1888 — January 14, 1961)

Actor Barry Fitzgerald was a major Hollywood star of the 1940s, nominated for both Best Actor and Best Supporting Actor for the same role as Father Fitzgibbon in 1944's *Going My Way.*

Newsmakers

Prince Edward, Earl of Wessex (March 10, 1964 —)

The third son of Elizabeth II of England and Prince Philip, Prince Edward is now seventh in line to the throne of sixteen countries.

Osama bin Laden
(أسامة بن محمد بن)
(عوض بن لادن)
(March 10, 1957 —
May 2, 2011)

Osama bin Laden was the founder of the jihadist organization al-Qaeda that claimed responsibility for the September 11 attacks on the United States, among man others. He was killed in a raid by US special forces in a covert operation in 2011.

Morgan Tsvangirai (March 10, 1952 —)

Morgan Tsvangirai is prime minister of Zimbabwe and a key figure in the opposition to President Robert Mugabe.

Kim Campbell (March 10, 1947 —)

In 1993, Kim Campbell became the 19th prime minister of Canada and the first female to hold that office.

James Earl Ray (March 10, 1928 — April 23, 1998)

James Earl Ray was convicted of the assassination of civil rights and anti-war activist

Dr. Martin Luther King, Jr. He died in prison. He confessed to the crime on March 10, 1969.

Tsar Alexander III of Russia (Александр Александрович) (March 10, 1845 — November 1 [O.S. October 20], 1894)

Known as Alexander the Peacemaker, Tsar Alexander III reigned as Emperor of Russia, King of Poland, and Grand Prince of Finland from 1881 until his death.

Space and Aviation

Laurel Clark (March 10, 1961 — February 1, 2003)

Navy captain and NASA astronaut Laurel Clark, MD., was killed in the Space Shuttle *Columbia* disaster.

Günther Rall (March 10, 1918 — October 4, 2009)

Luftwaffe pilot Günther Rall was the third most successful fighter ace in history, achieving 275 victories during World War II. He flew a total of 621 combat missions and was shot down 8 times.

Sports

Shannon Miller (March 10, 1977 —)

Gymnast Shannon Miller ranks as the most decorated gymnast, male or female, in U.S. history, with a total of seven Olympic medals.

Bobby Petrino (March 10, 1961 —)

Football coach Bobby Petrino was dismissed as head coach for the University of Arkansas in 2012 for failure to disclose an "inappropriate relationship" with a female employee.

Mitch Gaylord (March 10, 1961 —)

Gymnast Mitch Gaylord was the first American to score a perfect 10.00 in the Olympics, winning a gold, a silver, and two bronze medals in the 1984 Los Angeles Olympic Games.

Steve Howe (March 10, 1958 — April 28, 2006)

Rookie of the Year in 1980, All-Star in 1982, baseball player Steve Howe was suspended several times from the game for drug-policy violations. He died in a car accident in 2006.

Austin Carr (March 10, 1948 —)

Award-winning basketball player is known to Cleveland fans as "Mr. Cavalier."

Jim Valvano (March 10, 1946 — April 28, 1993)

Head basketball coach at NC State University, Valvano won the 1983 NCAA tournament, winning ACC Coach of the Year and the Arthur Ashe Award for Courage.

Spencer Gore (March 10, 1850 — April 19, 1906)

Cricket and tennis player Spencer Gore won the first Wimbleton Championship in 1877.

Who Died on March 10?

Acting

Cory Haim (December 23, 1971 — March 10, 2010)

A teen idol in 1980s Hollywood, known for his role in *The Lost Boys,* Haim struggled with drug addiction and died of pneumonia in 2010.

Richard Jeni (April 14, 1957 — March 10, 2007)

Stand-up comic and actor Richard Jeni was named to Comedy Central's list of the 100 Greatest Stand-ups of All Time. He also had a role in the Jim Carrey film *The Mask.*

Lloyd Bridges (January 15, 1913 — March 10, 1998)

Actor Lloyd Bridges appeared in more than 150 feature films and starred in the popular 1950s television series *Sea Hunt.* He is the father of actors Beau Bridges and Jeff Bridges.

Ray Milland (November 6, 1903 — March 10, 1984)

Actor Ray Milland won an Oscar for his role in 1945's *Lost Weekend* and played the murderous husband in *Dial M for Murder.*

June Marlowe (January 3, 1907 — March 10, 1986)

June Marlow played lovely schoolteacher Miss Crabtree in several *Our Gang* short subjects and appeared in numerous films of the silent era.

June Marlowe as "Miss Crabtree"

Historical Figures

Harriet Tubman (1820 — March 10, 1913)

Abolitionist and Union spy Harriet Tubman was born into slavery, escaped, and subsequently rescued more than 70 other slaves by means of the Underground Railroad. She led the Cumbahee River Raid, which freed more than 700 slaves, becoming the first woman to lead an armed expedition in the American Civil War. She was nicknamed "Moses" by abolitionist William Lloyd Garrison.

Jack Slade (January 22, 1831 — March 10, 1864)

Pony Express and stagecoach superintendent Jack Slade was instrumental in the opening of the American West, and became the archetype of the Western gunslinger. He was portrayed in Mark Twain's *Roughing It* as having killed 26 people, but only one is indisputable. A highly fictionalized movie of his life was made in 1953.

Harriet Tubman

Admiral George Elphinstone, 1st Viscount Keith (January 7, 1746 — March 10, 1823)

British admiral George Elphinstone was active throughout the Napoleonic Wars. He appears as a character in Patrick O'Brian's best-selling Aubrey-Maturin series of novels.

Letters

Zelda Fitzgerald (July 24, 1900 — March 10, 1948)

Wife of novelist F. Scott Fitzgerald, Zelda was known as "the first American Flapper." An icon of the Jazz Age and the Roaring Twenties, she wrote the semi-autobiographical novel *Save Me the Waltz*.

Mikhail Bulgakov (Михаи́л Булга́ков) (May 15 [O.S. May 3], 1891 — March 10, 1940)

Russian novelist and playwright Mikhail Bulgakov is best known for his novel *The Master and Margarita,* which has been called one of the masterpieces of the 20th century.

Music

Anna Moffo (June 27, 1932 — March 10, 2006)

Opera singer Anna Moffo was known as one of the leading lyric-coloratura sopranos of her generation, appearing with major opera companies worldwide.

LaVerne Baker (November 11, 1929 — March 10, 1997)

R&B singer LaVerne Baker had hits with "Tweedle Dee" (1955), "Jim Dandy" (1956), and "I Cried a Tear" (1958).

Andy Gibb (March 5, 1958 — March 10, 1988)

Teen idol and recording star Andy Gibb was the younger brother of Bee Gees Barry, Robin, and Maurice Gibb.

E. Power Biggs (March 29, 1906 — March 10, 1977)

Concert organist E. Power Biggs received a Grammy in 1986 for Best Chamber Music Performance.

Politics

Konstantin Chernenko (Константин Черненк) (September 24, 1911 — March 10, 1985)

Konstantin Chernenko was the fifth General Secretary of the Communist Party of the Soviet Union and Chairman of the Presidium of the Supreme Soviet, ruling the Soviet Union from 1984 until his death a year later.

Bull Connor (July 11, 1897 — March 10, 1973)

Segregationist Bull Connor was the Commissioner of Public Safety for Birmingham, Alabama, during the civil rights movement of th 1960s. He became an international symbol of bigotry for using fire hoses and police attack dogs against peaceful demonstrators, including children.

Jan Masaryk
(September 14, 1886 — March 10, 1948)

Czech diplomat Jan Masaryk made numerous broadcasts on behalf of the Czech government in exile during World War II. He served in the postwar Czechoslovakian communist-dominated government as foreign minister. He was found dead in 1948, an apparent suicide, but in 2004 the Prague police concluded that he had been assassinated, most probably at the order of the Kremlin.

Religion

Saint Marie-Eugénie de Jésus (August 25, 1917 — March 10, 1898)

Marie-Eugénie de Jésus founded the Religious of the Assumption in 1839. She was canonized in 2007.

Science

William Henry Bragg (July 2, 1862 — March 10, 1942)

Physicist and mathematician William Bragg shared the 1915 Nobel Prize in Physics with his son William Lawrence Bragg for their work in X-ray diffraction.

Sports

Barry Sheene (September 11, 1950 — March 10, 2003)

Barry Sheene was a British World Champion Grand Prix motorcyle road racer.

Bob Nieman (January 26, 1927 — March 10, 1985)

MLB outfielder Bob Nieman was the first player in major league history to hit two home runs in his first game.

The month of March, from the illuminated manuscript *Les Très Riches Heures du duc de Berry*

March: The Third Month

In ancient Rome, March was the first month of the year. As the first month of spring, in the Mediterranean climate it marked the beginning of the military campaign season. That's why March (Martius) is named in honor of Mars, the Roman god of war.

Although the first month of the year was moved back to January sometime during the transition of Rome from a kingdom to a republic (historians differ), March was the first month of the year in Russia until the end of the 15th Century, and is the first month of the year in many other cultures and religions.

In the northern hemisphere, March 1 marks the beginning of meteorological spring. In the southern hemisphere, March is the equivalent of September, making southern hemisphere March the beginning of autumn.

March is one of the seven months that have 31 days in it. March starts on the same day of the week as November every year, and except for leap years starts on the same day as February. March starts on the same day of the week as the previous June except for leap years, and in leap years starts on the same day as the previous September and December.

March in Other Cultures

In Finland, March is called *maaliskuu* (earthy month). In Ukraine, it's *березень* (birch tree). Other names for March include *Lentmonat* (Saxon), *Hyld-monath* (Angles), and *sušec* (Slovene).

March Symbols

Birthstones: Aquamarine and bloodstone, both representing courage.

Aquamarine

Birth Flowers Daffodils

Daffodils in Bagatelle Park, Paris, France

March Events

Honorary months: Presidents, Congresses, and nations around the world issue proclamations recognizing particular months to honor certain causes. These events generally fall in March. (All US unless otherwise noted.)

- National Nutrition Month

- American Red Cross Month

- Women's History Month (celebrated in Canada during October)

- Irish-American Heritage Month

- Colorectal Cancer Awareness Month

- Fire Prevention Month (The Philippines)

"March Madness": (United States) The NCAA Men's Division I Basketball Championship, popularly known as "March Madness" or the "Big Dance," is a single-elimination tournament to establish the champion college basketball team.

Multi-day events: Some March events span multiple days.

- **Nineteen Day Fast:** (Bahá'í Faith) March 2 through March 20

Movable events: Some events change dates from year to year.

- **Commonwealth Day:** Commwealth Day, formerly Empire Day, celebrates the establishment of the Commonwealth of Nations. It is marked by a service in Westminster Abbey and by a speech by England's monarch to the Commonwealht nations around the world. Commonwealth Day is held annually on the second

Monday in March, which can fall on any day between March 8 and March 14.

- **Canberra Day:** In the Australian Capital Territory, Canberra Day celebrates the official naming of Australia's capital city. It is also held annually on the second Monday in March, which can fall on any day between March 8 and March 14.

- **Passion Sunday:** The fifth Sunday of the Christian season of Lent is known as Passion Sunday in various Protestant denominations and by some traditionalist Catholics. Sometimes, the sixth Sunday of Lent is also known as Passion Sunday, but it is more commonly known as Palm Sunday. Passion Sunday starts the two week Passiontide, which ends on Holy Saturday, the day before Easter, commemorating the day that Jesus's body was laid in the tomb. The fifth Sunday of Lent can occur as early as March 8, and as late as April 11.

March Zodiac Signs

From the perspective of someone on Earth, the Sun appears to move through the sky throughout the year, along a path astronomers call the ecliptic plane. The ecliptic plane is divided into twelve constellations, known as the zodiac, based on traditionally observed patterns of stars. On your birthday, you can't see your constellation, because it's part of the daytime sky.

The zodiac was first developed by Babylonian astronomers about 2,500 years ago. Because they were unaware that the Earth wobbles like a spinning top (a motion known as *precession*), they didn't make allowance for the fact that the Sun's path through the zodiac changes over time.

That means there are now two sets of dates for your birth sign. The *tropical dates* are the original Babylonian dates; the *siderial dates* tell you where the Sun actually appears as it moves along its annual path.

March 10 is in Pisces in tropical dates, and is on the cusp of Aquarius and Pisces in siderial.

Aquarius

Tropical January 20 to February 19

Siderial February 12 to March 8 or 9 (as late as March 10 in leap years)

Aquarius is one of the oldest recognized constellations, originally representing the Babylonian god Ea. In Latin, Aquarius means "water-carrier," represented in its symbol. In Greek mythology, Aquarius is sometimes associated with Deucalion, who survived a world-cleansing flood. In Chinese astronomy, it is known as the Black Tortoise of the North (北方玄武, Běi Fāng Xuán Wǔ).

In astrology, Aquarius is considered to be masculine and extroverted, and despite the name is an air sign. Aquarians are supposed to be philanthropical, inventive, and individualistic.

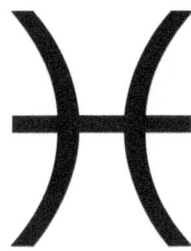

Pisces

Tropical February 20 to March 20

Siderial March 15 to April 14

In the Roman legend of Venus and her son Cupid, they escaped the clutches of Typhon, known as the "father of all monsters," by transforming into fish and tying themselves together with rope. That's why the name Pisces is plural for fish. The constellation appears as a somewhat ragged "V" shape, representing the rope, with the "fish" located at the two rope ends.

In astrology, Pisces is a water sign, compatible with the other water signs Cancer and Scorpio, as well as with the earth signs Taurus, Virgo, and Capricorn. Pisceans are supposed to be imaginative, compassionate, unworldly, secretive, and escapist.

What Day of the Week is March 10?

On what day of the week does March 10 fall?

Unfortunately, this isn't an easy question. Because the calendar year is 365 days long (366 in leap years), it doesn't divide evenly by the seven days of the week.

Also, the Earth goes around the Sun in about 365-1/4 days, so a calendar tends to drift over time. That's why the same date falls on different weekdays in different years.

This is made even more complicated by a change in calendars that took place in 1582. Our modern calendar has its roots in ancient Rome, in a calendar reform conducted by Julius Caesar. Caesar commissioned mathematicians to attack the problem, and came up with the idea of *leap years*, and thus standardized the calendar for centuries to come. This was called the *Julian calendar.*

Over time, however, the small errors in Caesar's calculation compounded. That's why Pope Gregory XIII commissioned the *Gregorian calendar*, used in most of the world today. Some countries converted in 1582, when the calendar was first developed; some converted later; others still haven't changed.

Gregorian and Julian aren't the only types of calendars. The Hebrew year, the Islamic year, and many other calendars are used in different parts of the world and among different people.

You can convert Gregorian dates to other calendars, including the Hebrew calendar, the Islamic calendar, and even the Mayan calendar by visiting the Fourmilab Calendar Converter at http://www.fourmilab.ch/documents/calendar/.

A 50-year brass perpetual calendar.

Copyright, Credit, and Contact

Follow Us

Our blog Dobson's Improbable History features short articles on events and people associated with each day, and updates several times each week. Get the latest on Twitter @SidewiseThinker.

Sources and Art Credits

All art and photographs are either in the public domain or used under a Creative Commons license. Attribution is provided where requested by the copyright owner or when of historical significance, listed below.

- The cover photograph of a GPO 332 Director telephone is by Dave Deben, who has released the image into the public domain.

- The 1892 photograph of Alexander Graham Bell on the telephone is from the Gilbert H. Grosvenor Collection at the Library of Congress Prints and Photographs Division, and is in the public domain because its copyright has expired.

- The portrait of Charles I of England was painted in 1632 by Daniël Mijtens, and is in the public domain because its copyright has expired.

- The 1906 illustration of the Courrières mine disaster is in the public domain because its copyright has expired.

- The photograph of Mahatma Gandhi at the spinning wheel is in the public domain because its copyright has expired.

- The photograph of Fulgencio Batista is from the Harris & Ewing Collection at the Library of Congress Prints and Photographs Division, donated under Instrument of Gift. No known restrictions exist on the use of this item.

- The FBI wanted poster of James Earl Ray is in the public domain as a work of the U.S. federal government.

- The photograph of the moons and rings of the planet Uranus were taken by the Hubble Telescope and are in the public domain as a work of the U.S. federal government.

- The illustration of the Mars Reconnaissance Orbiter is in the public domain as a work of NASA.

- The 2010 photograph of actor John Hamm is by Angela Natividad and is licensed under the Creative Commons Attribution-Share Alike 2.0 Generic license.

- The photograph of Carrie Underwood in concert was taken by "the_diet_starts_Monday" from Colorado, and is licensed under the Creative Commons Attribution-Share Alike 2.0 Generic license.

- The photograph of Bix Beiderbecke and the Wolverine Orchestra is in the public domain. It has been cropped for use here. The original can be found at http://commons.wikimedia.org/wiki/File:Wolverine_orchestra_1924.jpg.

- The photograph of Osama bin Laden is from the FBI "most wanted" list and is in the public domain as a work of the U.S. federal government.

- The portrait of Tsar Alexander III is by Nikolay Shilder, and is in the public domain because its copyright has expired.

- The screenshot of June Marlowe from the Our Gang short "School's Out" is in the public domain because its copyright was not renewed.

- The photograph of Harriet Tubman is in the public domain.

- The photograph of Jan Masaryk is from the Library of Congress Prints and Photographs Division and is in the public domain because its copyright has expired.

- The illustration of the month of March (used on the back cover and on page 41) is from the French Gothic illuminated manuscript *Les Très Riches Heures du duc de Berry* by the Limbourg Brothers, Jean Colombe, and an intermediate painter whose name is lost to history.

- The photograph of aquamarine has been released into the public domain.

- The photograph of daffodils is by Myrabella, and is licensed under the Creative Commons Attribution-Share Alike 3.0 Unported license.

- The 1917 Women's Suffrage demonstration comes from the Library of Congress, Prints and Photographs Division, LC-USZ62-31799 DLC

- The 50-year perpetual calendar photograph is in the public domain.